Lachlan Woods Photography

Jean Tong is a Melbourne-based writer and director creating politically irreverent works about the untidiness of cultural identification, structural inequality, and Otherness. Her work—tonally best described as 'wry outrage'—makes explosive statements using dark humour and vivid imagery that tends to burrow under the skins of audiences long after they leave the theatre. Her other work includes *macdeath: a coda*, *TERRORISM*, and *Romeo is Not the Only Fruit*. She has presented at the Emerging Writers' Festival and published in *Peril Magazine*. She is currently completing a Master in Writing for Performance at the VCA.

HUNGRY GHOSTS

Jean Tong

Currency Press
Sydney

CURRENCY PLAYS

First published in 2018
by Currency Press Pty Ltd,
PO Box 2287, Strawberry Hills, NSW, 2012, Australia
enquiries@currency.com.au
www.currency.com.au

Typeset by Dean Nottle for Currency Press.
Cover design by Celeste Njoo, Melbourne Theatre Company.
Cover photograph by Justin Ridler.
Cover photo shows Emina Ashman and Jing-Xuan Chan.

Currency Press acknowledges the Traditional Owners of the Country on which we live and work. We pay our respects to all Aboriginal and Torres Strait Islander Elders, past and present.

A catalogue record for this book is available from the National Library of Australia

Contents

these are monuments but what are we worshipping?

INTRODUCTION

'How long is a piece of string if you tie one end to your home country and the other to your heart?'

Jean Tong is a fiercely intelligent playwright with something to say. We first met when she was studying Arts at Melbourne University. I had been brought on as director's mentor on a short play she had written. What struck me about her writing was its rage and immediacy. Although at the time she wasn't yet in control of her craft, the text had a pulsing intensity and a desire to communicate something angry. Fast-forward five years, Jean has honed her craft and all those qualities endure—that rage has not abated one bit.

Hungry Ghosts deftly weaves together the Malaysian Airlines Flight 370 disaster, Malaysia's billion-dollar 1MDB scandal and the story of a Queer-Chinese-Malaysian Australian trying to find her place in the world. By intersecting these three narrative threads, Tong insistently interrogates ideas of absence and identity, finding tension between desire and greed, family and nationhood. Sitting underneath is a pulsing rage for a country where corruption is endemic, an identity that cannot be fully expressed, a longing that will never be sated.

The longing is most explicitly represented by the MH370 disaster. Malaysia Airlines flight 370 was an international passenger flight that disappeared on March 8, 2014. The flight was scheduled to fly from Kuala Lumpur International Airport to Beijing Capital International Airport. It was carrying 12 Malaysian crew and 227 passengers from all over the world. While flying over the South China Sea the aircraft disappeared from air traffic control systems and military radar. Despite the most expensive multinational search in aviation history, the aircraft was never recovered. Two hundred and thirty nine souls lost, families unable to gain closure, Facebook and Twitter awash with 'thoughts and prayers'. In January 2017, almost four years later, the search was suspended with no conclusive findings. These souls are lost, forever searching, most likely victims of foul play. The idea of the searching lost soul is integral to the diasporic experience that Tong interrogates. It no accident that the play is titled *Hungry Ghosts*.

In Chinese Buddhism, hungry ghosts are beings driven by intense emotional needs and only manifest from tragedy or 'evil deeds'. Interestingly, if we go further back, in very early Chinese and Vietnamese mythology, hungry ghosts are those who have been false, deceitful, greedy people, and their karma is an insatiable hunger. Tong's *Hungry Ghosts* are seekers but they also exist in and embody corruption, another central tenet of the work.

'How many planes do you have to lose before people forget about the money you lost?'

The 1MDB Scandal (1 Malaysia Development Berhad), is a complicated, corrupt and bloody web of financial dealings involving Malaysian Prime Minister Najib Razak, that spans the globe. In short, Razak had been accused of channeling close to 700 million USD from 1MDB, a government-run strategic development company, to his personal bank accounts. 1MDB was created to boost Malaysia's economy. Razak denied allegations that he funneled public funds to his personal account, claiming instead they were large donations from undisclosed sources. The highest profile aspect of the 1MDB scandal is the financing of the box-office hit *The Wolf of Wall Street*, which was funded by Red Granite Pictures, a production company owned by Riza Aziz, Razak's stepson. It is alleged that millions of dollars was diverted from 1MDB to fund the film. No-one is left untouched by this corrupting element in the play. Even the audience becomes complicit, as consumers of the film and unwitting participants in a fraudulent system. The murder of Shaariibuugiin Altantuyaa—a Mongolian National who worked for Razak—is at the epicentre of this corruption thread in *Hungry Ghosts*. Altantuyaa was employed as a translator for then Defence Minister, Abdul Rasak Baginda, and they became romantically involved. It is reported that Altantuyaa discovered one of the parties involved in negotiations to purchase submarines from France for the Malaysian government paid out commissions of €114 million, which were subsequently credited in the accounts of Baginda. A letter written by Altantuyaa (found after her death) shows that she had been blackmailing Baginda to remain silent about her knowledge of the deal. The Malaysian police found fragments of bone (later verified as belonging to Altantuyaa) in the Malaysian forest. She had been shot twice before C4 explosives blew up her remains. Just like the lost souls from flight MH370, Altantuyaa is lost (her DNA literally obliterated) and Malaysia itself lost in a quagmire of scandal and corruption.

In an interview with Melbourne Theatre Company, Tong expressed how the three narratives clicked for her when she realised:

> 'The nature of grasping at straws during a tragedy, the scale of the financial operations and volume of assets, my physical distance from home and inability to fully contribute to the discussions that were unfolding about the country's socio-politics—it fell into place so suddenly. I noticed that the common thread seemed to be a sense of loss, or an inability to speak due to either the suppression or lack of knowledge, or the wistful melancholy for something missing.'

Formally, *Hungry Ghosts* is a collection of scenes, events and monologues using multiple languages, modes and tones, which all refract and relate to its central idea of what it is to be unexplained, forgotten, to exist in the liminal—to be 'ghosts'. The lack of traditional narrative allows the audience to make their own meaning from the disconnected scenes and moments. The specificity of material does not push its audience away—quite remarkably it grounds the work and makes it relatable on so many levels.

In the first scene of the play, 'Animal Kingdom', Tong uses the metaphor of pistol shrimp to unpack the idea of how one small lone voice, although lost in a vacuum, can have a large impact on the world around it. The pistol shrimp is a small crustacean that creates a bubble of nothingness, a void, when it snaps its claw shut. This tiny bubble is suspended in the middle of the ocean until it explodes and the ocean crashes back in to fill the void. The noise that colonies of these shrimp make is so loud that it interrupts military and scientific sonar. A lone voice then asks:

> 'I wonder what it's like in that bubble. In that absolute quiet, in the silence of a million waves, billions of networks of oceanic activity. Imagine that peace. It stretches on forever, a silence

where anything can happen. I could be anyone. Do anything. I could hide in that silence. I could become something in that silence. I could weaponise myself, kill a king. I could make myself the greatest, most invisible danger of the big blue sea wrapped in a tiny, tiny, shrimp body. And then the moment passes, and the great crushing weight of the ocean whooshes back in.'

Tong proposed, when introducing *Hungry Ghosts* to the Melbourne Theatre Company subscribers at the 2018 launch that:

'People are increasingly discovering highly specific ways of identifying themselves and figuring out how to talk about the way they experience the world. I'm really interested in the outliers of these categories—when and why do these labels fail, and what other expectations come with those new identities or categories? Language is intoxicatingly powerful, but incredibly slippery: who are we with it, and who are we without it? I hope that my writing opens up some spaces on all of those levels.'

Tong opens up a quantum space in this first scene to tackle the biggest mystery, our own existence—Who are we? What is our true nature? In the realm of quantum physics there is no matter. What we think of as matter are tiny particles that are waves of potential—different potential outcomes of reality with infinite possibilities. Space and time exist within (rather than without) the quantum space. *Hungry Ghosts* exists in this quantum space, underneath the waves, inside the bubble, in the absolute quiet, where anything can happen. It is at once a love/hate letter to Malaysia and a meditation on who we are, in the silence.

Jean Tong is part of a new wave of writers and performance makers finding their way to our main stages. Over the past few years, I have had the privilege of directing a number of works written by artists from diverse backgrounds. These works all share an investigation around identity and belonging in relationship to the dominant culture. They have all used multiple languages as a tool to expose their audiences to ways of seeing, feeling and interpreting fluid identities. These perspectives on our stages allow some audience members a new lens through which to see the world, and affirm and celebrate the experience of previously ignored audiences. I can only hope that with the inclusion of stories like these (and many others around the country) on our main stages, we will increasingly see more diversity embedded in the dominant cultural narrative. Tong's work is an important voice in this growing conversation.

Petra Kalive

Petra Kalive directed *Hungry Ghosts* for Melbourne Theatre Company in 2018.

NOTES

hungry ghosts can be performed by a minimum of three performers. Casting *must* be diverse.

Line allocations have been indicated in this script, but where appropriate, these can be changed at the discretion of each performance.

/ indicates where the next speaker interrupts or joins in.

Scene titles can be projected, read out by performers, pre-recorded, or discarded. Productions can use all, some, or none of the scene titles in performance. The titles should inform the meaning of each scene.

English translations of the Malay and Mandarin lines have been provided, but anything written in a language other than English should be delivered as written, or in another language other than English. The translations and other information provided in the footnotes can be delivered in production—how this might be done is not specified.

References/quotations in the text draw from a range of sources, in particular the *Wall Street Journal* investigation into the 1MDB lawsuit. Where possible, these sources have been referred to in the footnotes accompanying the text.

Italicised dialogue, appearing on pages 9, 40–42 is quoted from the movie The Wolf of Wall Street *(2013) and can be played as video, performed live, as voiceover et cetera.*

Hungry Ghosts was first performed by Melbourne Theatre
Company at the Southbank Theatre, The Lawler, Melbourne,
on 3 May 2018, with the following cast:

> Emina Ashman
> Jing-Xuan Chan
> Bernard Sam

Director, Petra Kalive
Set Designer, Eugyeene Teh
Costume Designer, Sophie Woodward
Lighting Designer, Emma Valente
Composer, Sound Designer, Darius Kedros

A minimum of three performers, unnamed.

PRE-SHOW: ANIMAL KINGDOM

PROJECTION: A video made up of montages of the deep sea, various weird fish and pistol shrimp is projected onto an empty stage while the audience enters. The video is a little scruffy and homemade. The crackling sounds of pistol shrimp clicking underwater.

1:    The pistol shrimp is a species of crustacean that only grows to about three to five centimetres long, but competes with sperm whales for noisiest animal in the ocean. Colonies of pistol shrimp generate so much background noise that they misdirect military and scientific sonar used to detect underwater objects.

3:    One of their claws, a snapper over half the size of its body, makes this noise.

1:    When this snapper slams shut, it creates a cavitation bubble— a literal cavity, a void, a millisecond of nothingness, a vacuum suspended in the middle of the ocean—that explodes when the rest of the ocean rushes back to fill that rip.

2:    I wonder what it's like in that bubble. In that absolute quiet, in the silence of a million waves, billions of networks of oceanic activity. Imagine that peace. It stretches on forever, a silence where anything could happen. I could be anyone. Do anything.

I could hide in that silence. I could become *something* in that silence. I could weaponise myself, kill a king. I could make myself the greatest, most invisible danger of the big blue sea wrapped in a tiny, tiny, shrimp body.

And then the moment passes, and the great crushing weight of the ocean whooshes back in.

SCENE: TELL-ALL 1

2:    Hi.

Sorry, I've been really busy.

Listen, I have to run soon but—

No, everything's fine.

It's six-thirty, daylight savings, two hours, yeah.

Yeah, I've eaten.

I called because—

No, no, it's fine, I didn't get hit by a car—

Listen, listen, can you just—

Hello, can you hear me?

Yeah, it's just about the trip, I—

Yeah, it's just been really

I think I have to, I won't be able to, I can't quite get time off, so I

Yeah, I don't know when I can

Sorry

Listen, I actually have to go but—

Yeah yeah yeah. We'll talk soon.

Sorry. Again.

Bye, love you. Bye.

SCENE: TRAGEDY PORN

1:    It's a bird

3:    It's Superman

2:    It's a plane, fuckhead

3:    There are people

1:    The people are burning the plane

3:    My people are burning because of the plane

1:    I could've been on that plane

3:    I wish I'd been on that plane

1:    I was almost on that plane

2:    I was nineteen

1:    I *was* on that plane. No-one was screaming. By the end, no-one was screaming.

3:    Hypoxia—

1:    Depressurisation of the cabin, which knocks you out into a happy unconsciousness within thirty seconds

3:    Freezing white mist swirling in the aisles and ice crystals on eyelashes

1:    A jungle of oxygen masks over quiet bodies.

2:    Or: everyone was screaming

3:    Fire.

1:    It started in the cockpit, knocked out all systems

3:    It spread so quickly, smoke and temperature so high you couldn't even cry for your tears drying up.

2:    Or: a calculated disappearing act. The pilot—

1:    Captain Zaharie Ahmad Shah

3:    —taking a detour over the Malacca Strait to take one last look at his home island, Penang, before pulling a disappearing act. Revenge, in some small-big way, for the disappearing act his ex-wife pulled on him.

2:    Or: landing on a tiny strip of land in Diego Garcia, a small island in the Indian Ocean. A small island from which 1,579 people were disappeared in 1971 to make way for a United States military base.

1:    Or: terrorism. No groups stepped forward to claim credit. An accident, or genius? A hijacking of pure terror. You can't condemn who you don't know.

3:    Or: insurance fraud. Can't sue me if you can't find me.

2:    I wasn't on that plane.

1:    I just heard about it.

3:    I just wrote a memoir about it.

2:    I just listened to the silence ooze into the control booth, listened to everyone around me listen to the quiet crackling radio silence.

1:    I *was* on that plane and when it went down I held a stranger's hand and looked into their eyes and either she was weeping or I was weeping because suddenly all I could see was water everywhere.

3:    I couldn't see it but I could hear it.

1:    The screaming.

3:    The crying.

1:    The praying.

3:    The silence in the cabin when metal shrieked and tore itself apart on impact.

2:    I want to say there was something beautiful in the rhythm of the windows cracking, then shattering.

1:    I want to say there was something tragically funny about some kid's stuffed rabbit hurtling past my head, caught by gravity out of a limp grip.

3:    I want to say there was a sadness in the way clothes streamed out of cargo and floated past curious aquatic sea creatures who rummaged around with blunt teeth and ethereal limbs, weird fish with fucked-up faces and no eyelids.

2:    I want to say all of that.

3:    Paint that picture.

1:    Paint *a* picture.

1/2/3:   It could have been

2:    a fire.

1:    an accident.

3:    terrorists.

2:    It could have been plucked out of the sky by a benevolent god who needed something to distract her son with while she paid for a venti triple cream mocha Frappuccino.

1:    It probably wasn't any of those things.

3:    It was just bad luck

1:    Shit happens

3:    People die

1:    Statistically, travelling by plane is safer than going out for Friday night drinks

2:    You know what I think about a lot? Electronic beeping, the kind that's automatic and doesn't ever stop because the machine thinks that it's telling you all kinds of important information.

I think about that kind of beeping when I think about the plane, about MH370, about its detour to the bottom of the ocean, about it being under huge amounts of pressure but somehow managing to stay intact, against all odds. About its cabin full of people, dead on impact but also, against all odds, intact. And there's just this persistent beeping, beep, beep, beep, beep, beep, from the fridge up in First Class, reminding you that if you want to keep the champagne fresh, keep the party going, you just have to get to the door before it's too late. You just have to follow the beeping and find the door.

Pause.

3:    I don't buy it.

1:    I don't believe it.

3:    I can't see it.

2:    It's not impossible though.

3:    A little improbable.

1:    Not implausible.

3:    Is it likely though?

1:    Likely that that plane, on a standard trip from Kuala Lumpur International Airport to Beijing Capital International Airport, took a bit of a detour and went in exactly the wrong direction, avoided detection of all experienced aviation controllers and on-board crew, landed in the middle of the Indian Ocean and sank, yielding not one body, not one piece of oversized luggage?

3:    It's not *likely*.

2:    But it's not impossible.

1:    I mean, it happened.

2:    Didn't it?

1:    Three hundred tons of metal, Boeing 777, two hundred and twenty-seven passengers, twelve crew members.

3:    Somewhere on its six-hour journey from KL to Beijing.

1:    So many lives, lost.

2:    So many living, grieving.

3:    A corporation that never recovered.

1:    A big fucking tragedy.

3:    Mystery.

1:    Lost plane.

3:    Lost people.

1:    Lost money.

2:    Lost person.

1:    Just.

2:    Gone.

1:    Dead?

2:    Gone.

1:    But dead?

3:    What's the difference?

1:

2:    Gone.

SCENE: TALES

1:    It's a loss

3:    It's a profit margin

2:    It's embezzling, fuckhead

1:    Prime Minister Najib Razak

3:    He was twenty-three when he was first elected as a member of parliament

2:    681 million USD

1:    Twenty-five years old when he became Deputy Minister of Energy, Telecommunications and Post

3:    Youngest Deputy Minister in the country

2:    681 million USD

3:    Twenty-nine years old when he became Chief Minister of Pahang

1:    Youngest Chief Minister in the country

2:    How do you lose that much money?

1:    Age thirty-three, 1986

3:    Minister of Culture, Youth and Sport

2:    So close.

1:    Age thirty-eight, 1991

3:    Minister of Defence

2:    So close.

1:    Age forty-two, 1995

3:    Minister of Education

2:    The year I was born.

3:    Age forty-seven. 2000

1:    Minister of Defence, again.

3:    Did they run out of women, or?

2:    I wonder what it's like in that bubble.

1:    You could be someone in that bubble.

3:    You could be the greatest visible danger of the country.

1:    But.

3:    Finally.

2: Finally.

3: 2004.

1: Deputy Prime Minister.

3: So close you could taste it.

1: So close you could be it.

2: Then:

3: 2008, Finance Minister.

2: How many ministry positions do you have to have held before you know what power really means?

3: Before you can taste it?

1: Before you can be it?

2: 2009.

1: Prime Minister.

2: How do you lose that much money?

3: Earn

1: Take

2: How many planes do you have to lose before people forget about the money you lost?

3: Take

1: Earn

3: It could've been—

2: How many corrupt state officials generating headlines about bigger things does it take to distract lawyers

1: Corporations

3: PetroSaudi International

1: Goldman Sachs

3: Hollywood

1: Nations

3: British Virgin Islands

1: Abu Dhabi

3:      America

1:      Switzerland

3:      Malaysia

1:      The world

2:      1.26 billion USD

3:      How many search parties does it take to locate a missing plane?

> 'You know what a "Fugayzi" is?'
> '"Fugazi".'
> 'It's a fake.
> 'Fairy dust.'
> 'It doesn't exist.'

1:      How do you lose that much money?

2:      Three billion USD

1:      How many plane crashes does it take to shake an accusation of corruption?

2:      How do you lose something that big?

3:      Take

1:      Earn

2:      What's the difference?

1:      How much money would a corrupt state official embezzle if a state official could officially be corrupt?

3:      Itsy, bitsy spider, climbed up the water spout. Out came the rumours washed the spider out. Down came the plane and dried up all the rain, so the itsy, bitsy spider went up the spout again.

2:      How long is a piece of string if you tie one end to your home country and the other to your heart?

SCENE: FAMILY DINNER 1

1:      Do you ever think about Prime Minister Najib Razak as a family man?

Really, just think about it.

Him and his wife Rosmah and stepson Riza sitting around a big long dinner table.

2:    A bigger, longer dinner table than this one

1:    I wonder what she calls him. Jib? Jib-ster? Jibby?

2:    That's good.

1:    She's definitely a scary matriarch.

I can imagine her just standing at the bottom of the stairs screaming that up the stairs.

2:    *JIIIIB!*

1:    Najib flinching and getting a papercut on his dick from the hundred-ringgit notes laid out all over the bed he's rubbing himself on.

2:    Riza accidentally ripping his little baggie of coke open with a little puff of powder everywhere, giving him the white face he's always wanted.

1:    When he tries to get downstairs, he gets stuck because he keeps trying to *push* open his bathroom door.

2:    I wonder if Rosmah knows why Riza keeps getting nosebleeds.

1:    Let's be real, he was snorting tiny diamonds by the time he was three years old.

3:    You're gonna get us arrested.

2:    What? Is eating illegal here now?

1:    Can you imagine?

2:    No more *duit kopi*, how to drink *kopi* anymore?

3:    You two wanna face forty-three years like Zunar?

1:    *He's* an artist.

2:    *We're* just talking.

3:    Sedition is conduct or speech which incites people to rebel against the state

1:    sedition refers to elected state officials conducting themselves in a manner which incites people to rebel against the state

2:    sedition is speaking the unspeakable with great accuracy

1:    *I* think she cooks.

2:    *I* think she's cooking up another scheme to bankrupt the country *again*.

1:    How do you think they seat themselves around the table? Rosmah and Najib each at one end or just Rosmah at the head of the table and Najib and Riza on her left and right?

2:    Definitely Rosmah at the head of the table.

3:    Okay, but if they had a round table then who would be in charge?

2:    Chaos would reign.

1:    Riza can't stop rubbing his gums and sniffing—it's pretty gross, but Rosmah just assumes it's because the maids made the *sambal* too spicy again.

2:    Najib has it figured out, but only because Riza slipped him a shoebox full of neat little packets to take to the office in exchange for helping him pull open his toilet door.

1:    It's a good exchange. Najib has to keep his staff happy, somehow.

2:    Has to bring the nation to its knees willingly, quietly, somehow.

1:    Asking people to keep everyone else's mouths shut is no easy task.

2:    Finding the right people to put enough trust in that you could get them to take your clothes to the drycleaners, clothes covered in the blood of your country's people, is no easy task.

1:    It's a fine balance, figuring out how much to pay people when they're also your trusted friends.

2:    It's not an easy thing to arrest people first, before they arrest you.

1:    It's just not an easy thing to ask people to arrest their friends and family for saying anything that sounds even a little bit like *Najib is a fu—*

3:    He has to work *so much* to keep his wife happy, somehow.

1:    Rosmah could find someone better at any time.

3:    Wouldn't be hard.

2:    He's never home because he has to spend hours and hours and hours in the office keeping track of all this money pouring into his bank account.

1:    I'm so bad at maths, I'd hate having to do that.

3:    I mean, it's only addition so it wouldn't be that bad.

1:    Do you think Rosmah helps when it comes to calculating compound interest?

2:    She needs to know exactly how much money she can spend the next time she takes a private jet to Hermès, so probably.

1:    She just wants to make sure her son feels proud of her when she attends his big premieres.

2:    Riza's worked so hard too.

3:    Co-founding Red Granite Pictures with public funding.

1:    Art by the people, for the people.

3:    Not many people could manage to get 100 million USD out of their daddy's bank account without them noticing.

2:    Or maybe Rosmah did it for him and didn't tell Najib.

3:    Do you think they fought when Najib found out?

2:    Nah.

1:    No way.

2:    He probably went straight to Riza and scolded him for not knowing how to steal properly.

3:    I mean, what a conversation to have.

1:    What do you think they talk about?

3:    It got a little tense the last time someone said the name 'Altantuyaa' at the table.

2:    No-one wants to think about that

1:    No-one wants to think about

3:    blood under sheets

1:    blood under carpets

3:    carpets of leaves and branches rotted by bits of brain from a woman who—

2:    Altantuyaa

1:    No-one wants to think about her when they've got a spoonful of sambal in front of them

3:    That deep red chilli paste

2:    matted with onions and speckled with chilli seeds

1:    Everything comes with a price.

2:    I would hate to have to sit through their family dinners.

1:    I would *love* to have to sit through their family dinners.

3:    If I get placed on house arrest, I hope it's in their house.

1:    We'd get to see, *in person*, Rosmah at the head of the table, thinking about power, happy.

2:    Riza coked out of his head, happy.

1:    And Najib just sitting there, watching them both. He's always stressed out of his mind at work, but when he comes home, he gets to relax.

2:    He gets some time off to think about what it means to lie.

1:    To think about money, to think about what money can buy for his family, what money *has* bought for his family.

2:    He watches them eat.

1:    He doesn't eat much anymore.

3:    After you've consumed an entire nation and all its people, *nasi lemak* never quite tastes the same again.

2:    Everything comes with a price.

1:    Maybe he's happy too.

SCENE: FLIGHT

2:      The first set of people who voluntarily stepped inside a giant
        tin can to be violently thrust into the air and rocketed about
        the sky were brave.

1:      The first set of people who paid money for that pleasure were
        fucking idiots.

3:      When people say 'when hell freezes over', I show them a
        picture of a plane. All I can think about in that tiny seat is
        how much it smells like jet fuel and this other non-smell. It's
        like if a hospital had weird sterile afternoon sex with a petrol
        station and then refused to acknowledge it'd ever happened.

        People tell me they can't smell anything, but my gag reflex is
        pretty much flexing the entire plane ride. I'm the guy who sits
        there with his eyes closed, fists clenched and mouth fucking
        screwed shut. And yes, I will swallow the vomit back rather
        than open my eyes and struggle for the bag, thank you for
        asking, now please stop talking because I can confirm that it
        doesn't taste as good coming back up.

2:      If you've pre-booked the window seat like you should've, you
        get that big perfect view post-takeoff, when the plane first
        peaks through the sea of clouds and you could almost feel
        like you're swimming through this massive field of puffy
        vastness in that big big big big big blue clear sky. That one
        moment always feels like it stretches on forever, this peaceful,
        magnificent breach out into a sky that's usually just beyond
        your reach, but not today, not in that moment. Today, that
        moment between you and this peace stretches on forever. You
        could be anyone. Do anything.

1:      If someone else has pre-booked your personal private jet for
        you, using the taxes of the people you represent, you can
        settle back into your plush, comfortable seats and hold your
        perfectly sweating, sparkling guava juice in your hands and not
        worry about anything. You can close your eyes and a hot towel
        will lay itself over your eyes. Here, suspended miles above

the petty squabbles of your government, you're *someone*. Here, surrounded by your closest and most trusted, you can rest. Here, up in the clouds, snuggled into bodyguards and leather armrests, you're safe.

3:   Fact: everyone working on the plane is being paid to be nice to you.

2:   Fact: flying is heaven.

1:   Fact: flying is like taking a class on class struggle.

2:   When you're on a plane, everything looks better. Most things look better, feel better, from a distance: people in clubs, border control, cities. Out in the distance, all you get is the godlike view of thousands of people living out their lives on the ground. You're omnipresent without being present.

1:   The best thing about flying: landing at night. From that distance, you can't see your domestic tragedies. Safe from political squabbles, existential angst. Temporary freedom.

3:   If I can force my eyes open and hold the puke back as we're about to land, there's nothing quite like looking at a gorgeous, spread-out city to make me feel like I could call it home. From afar, I feel like I could call anywhere home.

2:   It's like I'm no-one. Like I could become anyone.

I could change, be a different person by the time I touch down.

I could do anything.

3:   I could hijack the plane.

1:   I could hijack a country.

2:   I could make myself the greatest, most invisible danger of that big, blue sky, wrapped in a fragile, airport-immigration-approved body.

3:   I could do anything.

SCENE: GOODNIGHT

2011/2014.

1:    Are you done packing? Don't forget your passport.

3:    We're going to be late, hurry up.

A: *Lumpur Control, this is MH three seven zero, good morning.*

B: *Good morning, MH three seven zero, Lumpur Control. Please taxi to holding point alpha one one runway three two.*

A: *Alpha one one runway three two, MH three seven zero copy that.*

1:    Fuck, I'm so sleepy. Maybe you should drive. Oh wait, you still don't have your licence. Loser. How are you going to get around Melbourne?

2:    Pretty sure there's public transport, asshole.

B: *MH three seven zero, runway three two right cleared for take-off.*

A: *Runway three two right cleared for take-off MH three seven zero copy that.*

1:    Traffic looks pretty bad but we'll probably be fine.

2:    I told you we should've left earlier.

1:    Maybe you should've taken less time stuffing your face.

2:    Maybe I don't know when I'm going to get *apam balik* for breakfast again.

1:    Drama queen. You know they have basically more Malaysians in Melbourne now than they do white people, right?

A: *Lumpur Control, MH three seven zero.*

C: *MH three seven zero, Lumpur Radar, good morning. Climb flight level two five zero.*

A: *Morning, flight level two five zero, MH three seven zero.*

2:    God, my passport photo looks like hell.

1:    The camera only captures an objective account of reality.

2:    Eat shit.

1:    Love you.

3:    Don't fight, you won't see each other for another ten months.

1: Thank God.

2: Rude.

C: *MH three seven zero, climb flight level three five zero.*

A: *Flight level three five zero, MH three seven zero.*

3: Call me when you arrive.

2: Ya.

3: Have a safe flight.

2: Ya.

A: *MH three seven zero, maintaining level three five zero.*

C: *MH three seven zero.*

3: Don't eat too much junk food.

2: Ya.

3: No smoking, no drugs.

2: Ya.

3: No drinking.

2: Uh-huh.

3: Don't forget to call.

2: Ya.

C: *MH three seven zero please contact Ho Chi Minh City one two zero decimal nine for changeover. Goodnight.*

A: *Copy that. Goodnight.*

3: Love you so much. Bye.

2: Bye.

Love you too.

SCENE: BLOOD NOSES

2: I spent years digging my own grave

1: I was taught to speak myself six feet into the ground, to craft my own coffin in perfect metre

3: I was taught to love how perfectly I fit into that coffin

2: I was taught to love foreign books

1: Foreign clothes

3: Foreign debt

1: Foreign furniture

3: Foreign food

1: Foreign dance

3: Foreign songs

1: Foreign lands

3: Foreign people

1: Foreign piss

2: I was taught to love foreign and hate 'us'

1: I spent years unbending my own graces

3: Speaking words that felt real but meant nothing

2: Speaking in a language that meant killing something inside every time it fell out of my mouth

1: Speaking through a body that didn't belong to me

3: A body that never belonged to me

2: No-one knows how to cut the umbilical cord between you and your mother country

3: Although everyone who leaves tries

1: And tries

3: And tries

2: It was Thursday the day I left the country

1: It was dark

3: It was warm

2: I was sixteen

3: It was raining so hard the roads started to flood and for a second I didn't know how I'd feel if I actually missed my flight

1: My mother was crying

3: My father was crying

2: I was filled with so much hope I thought I might burst out laughing so hard that I would faint so I learnt to stamp down the hope and keep it quiet and then never stopped

1: I don't remember much about the goodbye because it was the first of many goodbyes

2: I don't remember much about the goodbye because I never say the words out loud

3: I remember every single farewell with absolute clarity. The trip to the airport always felt too short even if there was two hours of traffic hell, and the queue at the check-in line always felt empty even if it was packed. I remember walking to the departure gate with increasingly smaller steps until we're barely moving. I remember avoiding your hands because I was afraid I would never let go. I remember the strength in your back, your breath carefully even so you wouldn't cry and make it harder on me. I remember so clearly that when I wake up with the tendrils of that memory clinging to my eyelids I don't know whether to call it a dream or a nightmare.

1: No you don't. You don't remember a thing. You don't remember a single thing about a single farewell.

3: Well.

1: No-one's ever driven you to the airport. You've taken taxis every single trip. You've never had anyone wave to you as you walk through departure gates towards immigration officers who're so bored they almost wish you were a terrorist so they'd have something to do, finally. You've never had anyone to look back at one last time.

3: Well.

1: You don't remember shit.

3: Well. If I had anything to remember, that's what I'd remember.

1: You've never had someone say

2: 'Stay'

1: 'Please'

2: 'I miss you already'

1:    Or not say that.

3:    It doesn't really matter.

2:    No-one *really* means it when they ask you to stay

1:    You tell yourself

2:    Or they do mean it, but they know you'll still leave, you always do

3:    You've established a precedent

1:    A time limit that everyone's aware of

3:    There's only so much 'spending time together' you can handle

2:    Leaving is such sweet sorrow

3:    You could get high off sorrow

1:    It lingers

2:    That sweet, sweet, sweet sorrow of parting

1:    People missing you because they haven't had enough time with you to get sick of you

2:    Your presence will always be a bit of a novelty

   3: How've you been?

   1: So glad to have you back.

   3: So good to see you home.

   1: We've missed you.

   3: Have you lost weight? You look great.

   1: You look great. Have you gained weight?

   3: How was the flight?

   1: Was the pilot hot?

   3: Did you bring me anything from Australia?

   1: Did you bring back anything besides your stupid accent?

   3: Did you remember to turn off the fridge?

   1: Lock the windows?

   3: Have you met your nephew? Yeah, he's pretty big now.

1: Your clothes are in the back room—we needed more space.

3: Your cousin-sister got accepted to Imperial, she starts in September. No, she left three weeks ago to start settling in. She just didn't want to distract you since you were neck-deep in assessments. Yeah, big farewell party.

2: You've never stayed anywhere long enough to lay down any roots

1: Your friends are novelties too

3: People become abstract entities when they're far away

2: You become an abstract entity when you're far away

1: Each landing at a new airport is an exhilarating rush

3: Each time you breathe the country in you feel like you've arrived home

2: You know it won't last

3: Home is where the heart is

1: And the heart wants what the heart wants

3: Except when it doesn't know what it wants

2: 流连忘返 [liú lián wàng fǎn]: When staying feels so good you forget you have to leave.

3: I can't believe you didn't tell me you got a tattoo. Are you going to get another one? Did it hurt?

1: Did it hurt when you broke up with her?

3: When you found that old letter from your sister asking you to stop growing up so quickly?

1: When you stopped writing to your grandfather because you didn't know how to say 'gay' or 'softball' in Chinese

3: When they didn't tell you he got sick

1: When you didn't find out the house had been robbed until it was three weeks later and they'd put metal shutters in the house

3: When they say, 'You had to be there'

1: When they say, 'When are you coming back, we miss you?' and all you can do is get angry because otherwise you'll get sad

2: How long is a piece of string if you tie one end to your home country and the other to your heart?

1: Would you rather have been born into any other life?

3: Would you rather be monolingual?

1: Would you rather be a citizen of a place that's only ever seen peace and diplomatic relations with neighbouring countries?

3: Would you rather you'd been raised on a diet of meat pies and vegemite?

1: Would you rather sincerely believe in egalitarianism, that your birthplace and who your birth parents are doesn't predetermine, predestine the person you'll be, the life you'll live?

3: Would you rather have lived never knowing what being different, looking different, acting different feels like?

1: Would you rather look back at yourself and see only one reflection in the mirror?

3: Would you?

1: Would you have stayed, if you'd had a choice?

SCENE: THE WOLF ON OUR STREET

Dialogue from The Wolf of Wall Street *(2013) plays—refer to Justin Belfort's motivational speech (1:24:30–1:24:52).*

2: In the 2013 blockbuster, *The Wolf of Wall Street*, Leonardo DiCaprio plays Jordan Belfort, a stockbroker who goes from living the high life to being a low-life. He lies to a lot of people, lies *with* a lot of people, tries to lie low for a while, and then everything starts to unravel. Boy fucks up.

3: Fucks a lot of women, fucks up his nasal passages, fucks up his family. A classic, family-friendly summer hit.

1:      The word fuck, fucker, fucking, motherfucker and so on
        are used about five hundred times in the film, which is the
        most times those variations are used in a mainstream, non-
        documentary film.

2:      *The Wolf of Wall Street* was produced by Red Granite Pictures, an
        independent production company co-founded in 2010 by Riza
        Aziz, Prime Minister Najib Razak's stepson.

3:      Co-founded with public funding.

1:      Art by the people, for the people.

2:      Red Granite Pictures

3:      A red, round smear around a company heading

2:      Blood under

1:      Images can be deceiving

3:      Representation can be deceiving

1:      You can paint a picture and not know the truth you tell with it

3:      You can make a logo and not realise it's a confession

2:      Red Granite Pictures

1:      Blood on carpets of leaves

3:      Blood on gravelly roads

1:      On granite

2:      Pictures of big, red smears

3:      The big picture

1:      The Pictures: A Hollywood Smear; Big, Red, Bloodied Marks
        everywhere

2:      Red Granite Pictures

3:      Investigators believe that 238 million USD from 1MDB

1:      Public funding

3:      was sent to a bank account held in the name of Red Granite
        Capital Limited

2:      Riza Aziz.

3:   Investigators believe that 94 million USD of that sum was
     used to fund Riza Aziz's real estate habit.

1:   Investigators also believe that over 100 million USD was
     directed into Red Granite Pictures for the making of *The Wolf
     of Wall Street*.

3:   Art by the people, for the people.

1:   Red Granite Pictures gifted Marlon Brando's Oscar—a lump of
     metal worth approximately 600,000 USD—to Leonardo DiCaprio.

2:   Gold bars for gold stars.

1:   Leo has since turned over this Oscar to the authorities.

3:   In 2016, the US Department of Justice froze the flow of profits
     from *The Wolf of Wall Street*, and is now demanding the recovery
     and forfeiture of all assets made through illegal financial
     dealings.

1:   In 2017, Red Granite Pictures reached a settlement deal with
     the US government that would resolve claims against two other
     films made by the company.

3:   But not the claims against *The Wolf of Wall Street*

1:   and not the claims against Riza Aziz.

2:   Is this life imitating art, or art imitating life?

SCENE: TESTIMONY

1:   *Hari ini kita menerima reality.* [Today we accept reality.]
     Yang berlaku ini, ia ketentuan Allah. [Because it is determined by
     Allah.]

3:   We are grateful to all organisations and countries leading the
     extensive search operations, and our thoughts and prayers
     are with all the families of the passengers and crew of Flight
     370. Our family appreciates all wellwishes but now we ask for
     privacy, and request that our wish for solitude be respected
     during this time.

2:   … 我们知道这个消息的时候, [. . . last night when we heard
     the news,]

大家还是觉得还是不要相信政府. [in the end we felt that we should not believe the government.]

没有得到官方确认之前, 还没有得到
所有媒体的, 真正专家的, [Without getting official confirmation and all real expert opinions,]

我们都拒绝相信. [we refuse to believe it.]

3: I don't understand how the hell this happened. Every single board member of Malaysia Airlines should be held personally culpable for the slack response of the airline, for their denial of responsibility, for their disrespect of the families and loved ones involved. I want to sue them, I want to sue every slacker in the— Kick them out of the company, I want them to review their disaster-management response plan, I want every single person working that day to apologise, I want them to feel like. I want them to. How am I supposed to tell my mother that she has to bury her grandchildren without bodies, where do I put their clothes so their scent doesn't disappear, where do I put her unfinished manuscripts, the cereal only he eats? What am I supposed to do with their savings account, who am I supposed to support through university now, whose children am I supposed to cry over at graduation? If all of my children are gone and no-one is there to yell 'Ma!' up the stairs for me, am I still a mother? If I see their faces in my dreams, am I waking up *to* or *from* a nightmare?

2: 其实 , 有点不是很想再知道. [Actually, a part of me doesn't really want to know.]

肯定的是他们一定是去 … 去世了.[The sure thing is that they've . . . passed away.]

1: *Bagaimanapun, sekurang-kurangnya mesti ada bukti, kan?* [Shouldn't we have proof, at least?]

Kalau kerajaan kata kapal terbang dah berakhir di Lautan Hindi, [If the government can say that the plane ended up in the Indian Ocean,]
maka sekurang-kurangnya berikan bukti itu kepada kami lah! [then at the very least give us that proof!]

2:    我觉得的是，还有我家人觉得, [So I feel, and my family
      feels,]
      没什么要再问，没什么想知道的. [there's nothing we want to
      ask, nothing we want to know.]

1:    *Apa ia berani kata kapal terbang, kapal terbang yang sebesar itu dah hilang*
      sahaja tanpa sebarang bukti? adakah kerajaan fikir kami bodoh? [Do they
      dare to say that a plane that big just disappeared without any
      evidence? Does the government think we're stupid?]

2:    我们不已经出够事情了吗？ [Haven't we all been through
      enough already?]

3:    On January 17th, 2017, the search for MH370 which began
      in 2014 was officially suspended. Officials say that 'In the
      absence of new credible evidence it is not possible to continue
      searching' as 'every effort has been made'.

1:    In January 2018, a new private search by underwater survey
      company Ocean Infinity began. A US oceanographer and
      salvage expert claimed that if found, those aboard the plane
      will have been perfectly preserved, 'like a time capsule'.

3:    A jungle of oxygen masks over quiet bodies.

1:    The Malaysian government promised the Houston-owned,
      privately financed company up to 70 million USD if the plane
      is found within ninety days.

2:    Everything comes with a price.

A voiceover plays overhead.

1:    *Tuan-tuan dan puan-puan, kita telah mendarat di laparan terbang*
      antarabangsa KL. Bagi tujuan keselamatan, anda dikehendaki berada
      di tempat duduk sehingga isyarat 'pasangkan tali keledar' dipadamkan
      dan pesawat berhenti di sepenuhnya. Anda dibenarkan memasang telefon
      bimbit selepas isyarat 'pasangkan tali keledar' dipadamkan. [Ladies and
      gentlemen, we have landed at Kuala Lumpur International
      Airport. For security purposes, you must remain seated until
      the seatbelt sign has been turned off and the plane has come
      to a complete halt. You may turn on your mobile phones after
      the seatbelt sign has been turned off.]

3:     *Kepada warganegara kami mengucapkan Selamat Pulang dan kepada pelawat, kami mengucapkan Selamat Datang ke Malaysia.*

2:     To our visitors, *Selamat Datang* to Malaysia, and to Malaysians, welcome home. Thank you for flying with Malaysia Airlines, we look forward to seeing you again soon.

SCENE: FAMILY DINNER 2

The staging used in earlier scene Family Dinner 1 can be repeated in this scene.

1:     Do you ever think about Captain Zaharie Ahmad Shah as a family man?

3:     Forty-five thousand feet in the air

2:     He was fifty-three.

1:     Really, just think about it

       Him and his wife and kids sitting around a dinner table

2:     A dinner table like this one

3:     Hell, frozen over.

1:     Do you think his children were interested in planes?

2:     Do you think his wife felt lonely while he was away? Do you think she spent long, sleepless nights worrying about the unpredictability of weather patterns and secret flight paths of nuclear warheads?

3:     Do you think his children draw the Malaysian Airlines logo on the airplanes in their colouring books? Do you think they get told to open wide so the plane can make a landing on the runway of their tongues to deposit food in their mouths?

2:     If home is where the heart is, and his heart was in a different timezone, what time do you think he would've needed to have dinner to feel like he was back home?

1:     How do you think they seat themselves around the table?

2:

1:     Now.

2:

1:   How do you think they seat themselves around the table *now*.

3:   One chair even emptier than usual, not a temporary absence but a permanent one.

1:   One chair less at the table, just remove the evidence.

2:   Or:

1:   Empty chairs at empty tables.

3:   They don't even sit around the dining table anymore

1:   He'd probably hate the way they sit in front of the TV eating microwave dinners

3:   He'd had enough onboard microwave food to last him his entire lifetime

1:   He'd probably hate the way they sit in front of the TV eating silently in the glare and flicker of news programs telling them about alleged affairs he'd had

2:   Telling them 'truths'

3:   Telling them about the man their father—

1:   Husband—

3:   Is—

1:   Was—

2:   Telling them kernels spun out of thread spun into tales people cling onto so they can reassure themselves that the plane's disappearance hasn't knocked their entire world out of orbit

3:   Telling them their father did it on purpose

1:   By accident—

2:   It started in the cockpit

3:   That he was coerced—

1:   Bribed—

3:   Blackmailed—

2:   everyone was screaming

1:   Or:

2:   Or maybe the Lego pieces lie scattered on the floor

3: They used to sit together in the shape of an Imperial Star Destroyer but anything now that makes anyone think the words 'Unidentified Flying Object' just creates this big-small rip of dead silence in the middle of the living room

2: Maybe the TV's been unplugged since an accidental swing with a Wii remote shattered a row of LED bulbs in the set, leaving the screen unwatchable

1: They'd been playing Wii boxing because you can make the avatars look like whoever it is you need to punch in the face

3: It's a lot more fun than just doing it in the comfort of your own mind to the news anchors onscreen telling you all these lies

2: Truths—

3: About your father—

1: Husband—

3: They never talk about how hard his job is—

1: Was—

2: He'd spent 18,000 hours flying tens of thousands of people safely

That's 1,080,000 minutes worth of flying

1: 64,800,000 seconds worth of thinking

3: I wonder what he thought about

1: I wonder if he wondered if it was worth it

3: The money

2: What money?

3: What the money bought for his family

1: What the money could buy for his family

3: Security

1: Education

3: Escape

2: 64,800,000 seconds

3:   Those are some long, awkward silences if you don't get along
     with your co-pilot

1:   I would hate to be in that cockpit

3:   Hypoxia

1:   *'A deficiency in the amount of oxygen reaching your tissues.'*

2:   I imagine that that's what it would feel like on being told that

     3: Finding out that—

     1: Seeing on the internet that—

     3: Hearing on TV that—

     1: Being sent a text message that—

          3: 'MH370—

          1: lost contact—

          3: signal—

          1: tracking flight path—

          3: abruptly ended in the—

          1: ocean—

          3: lost—

          1: disappeared—

          3: presumed—

          1: lost'

2:   I imagine that that would feel a lot like hypoxia

1:   A deficiency in the amount of oxygen reaching your—

SCENE: A FAVOUR

1:   2009. Prime Minister Najib Razak launched 1Malaysia
     Development Berhad, 1MDB, the Malaysian national wealth
     fund.

3:   This launch was preceded by a meeting on board a yacht
     between Prime Minister Najib Razak, Malaysian financier Jho
     Low, and PetroSaudi CEO Tarek Obaid.

1: These actions should not in any event be construed as an act of corruption.

2: I was fourteen.

3: The national wealth fund 1MDB was established to drive 'strategic investment on behalf of the people of Malaysia'. Its establishment as a public trust fund should not in any event be construed as an act of corruption.

1: Expediting the processing time of vast amounts of public taxes

3: *duit kopi*

1: from the people of Malaysia to private individuals

3: for example, the CEO of PetroSaudi

1: in exchange for a 'nominal fee' should not in any event be construed as an act of corruption.

3: 681 million USD being 'gifted' back from private Saudi bank accounts to Prime Minister Najib Razak on behalf of the people of Malaysia should not in any event be construed as an act of corruption.

2: On behalf of the people of Malaysia: how do you gift that much money?

3: The sovereign wealth fund then generating 11 billion US dollars in public debt on behalf of the people of Malaysia should not in any event be construed as an act of corruption.

1: The accumulated debt resulting in the erosion of trust from foreign investors and devaluation of local currency thanks to Prime Minister Najib Razak's foray into driving strategic investment on behalf of the people of Malaysia should not in any event be construed as an act of corruption.

2: Everything comes with a price.

3: You scratch my back, I scratch yours.

1: 2002. Najib was still Defence Minister.

3: Najib's aide at the time was defence analyst Razak Baginda.

1: In 2002, Razak Baginda went to France to negotiate the purchase of two submarines for the Malaysian government.

3:    Altantuyaa was a Mongolian interpreter who'd lived all over the world and was fluent in Mongolian, Russian, Chinese, and English.

1:    Razak Baginda wanted an aide.

3:    Altantuyaa could speak French.

1:    She had no husband.

3:    But she did have two kids living in Mongolia with her parents.

2:    You scratch my back, I scratch yours.

3:    Which is what Baginda said to her when he started an affair with Altantuyaa.

1:    Maybe.

3:    And it's what Baginda said to the French submarine company about his commission fee.

1:    Or at least, that's what he thinks he said with Altantuyaa as his mouthpiece.

3:    Not speaking comes at a price.

1:    It's what Altantuyaa said when she asked for 500,000 USD to keep her mouth shut about both things.

3:    Maybe.

2:    She was pregnant.

1:

3:    It's what Baginda said to Najib when he asked for help getting rid of her.

1:    Everything you want comes with a price.

3:    It's what Najib's personal bodyguards said when they shot Altantuyaa in the head, carried her into the middle of the jungle, and blew her up using restricted military explosives so that the only credible evidence left of her was her DNA they scraped off rotting leaves.

1:    Where do you find that much military-restricted explosive?

2:    Altantuyaa

1:      blood

3:      leaves

1:      bits of blown-up brain

2:      Gone.

1/2/3: should not in any event be construed as an act of corruption.

1:      You scratch my back, I scratch yours.

3:      Everything in this country comes with a price.

2:      An act of corruption should not in any event be construed as an act of corruption if the act of corruption is not initially intended as an act of corruption although in the event of love becoming a part of the corruption such as if one loves corruption then the act of corruption is the act of love and the act of love becomes an act of corruption on behalf of the people of Malaysia and should therefore not in any event be construed as an act of corruption.

SCENE: REMEMBER WHEN

2:      people sometimes talk about what they were doing 'at the time'

        3: 'at the time' I was hanging up my clothes

        1: 'at the time' I was watching the latest episode of—

        2: at the time I was nineteen

3:      they've usually made these things up

1:      people have shit-arse memory, usually

3:      I can't even remember what I had for dinner last night

1:      I forgot my sister's birthday

3:      I remembered my brother's birthday but forgot to get him a present

1:      Every three months I forget my Facebook password.

2:      So we make it up

1:      It's not malicious or anything

3:     It's not for attention

1:     It's not out of disrespect

2:     reality just doesn't sound that good when it's retold

3:     if you're going to immortalise a memory

1:     better make it pleasant

3:     better make it pleasurable

2:     I remember therefore I am

3:     how did I remember to remember?

2:     people talk about what they were doing 'during' so they don't
       have to talk about

1:     after

2:     they go back to when they first heard about it

       1: 'I cried'

       3: 'I was in shock'

       1: 'I called my mum'

       3: 'I called my dad'

       1: 'I wanted to know they were okay'

       3: 'I wanted them to know that I loved them'

       1: 'that I forgave them'

       3: 'that I should've tried harder to save them from themselves'

       1: 'that I owed them that much'

       3: 'that family means family'

       1: 'no matter what'

2:     because after

1/3:   'AFTER'

2:     is like a bad dream

3:     will they pick up the phone?

1:     Won't they?

2:     After is how you can judge someone's personality

1: You don't know what someone's really made of until you watch the way they respond to tragedy

3: To panic

1: To the Worst Case Scenario

3: To hell, frozen over

2: After is like going on holiday with your latest partner for two weeks

1: Make or break

3: After tells you which path to take

1: After is:

2: TWITTER: #MH370 thoughts & prayers please come home I love you be safe please

1: After is:

2: FACEBOOK: thoughts & prayers #MH370

3: After is

1: YOUTUBE: devastated for the families affected by MH370, please add your thoughts and prayers to the comments

2: I wish I'd said it before they

1: After is

2: After is what didn't happen

3: Couldn't happen

1: Won't ever happen

2: After is everything I didn't get to say

3: After is everything you did say and wish you hadn't

1: After is not being able to think at all

3: After is dry eyes while everyone else manages to sob their numbness away

2: After is the relief you can't talk about, because no-one knew about the. and if you're the only one who remembers the. did it ever happen?

3:    After is after

1:    After is always *over*

2:    But the problem with that is that we find the concept of finality

1:    Really

3:    Really

1:    Really

3:    Hard to grasp

2:    So we make it up

1:    Pause the moment in amber

3:    Suspend it forever

2:    Let it be something that will still be there After

1:    Who cares about the truth anymore?

2:    How can there be truth in a post-truth world?

3:    How can there be truth after a tragedy?

1:    How can there be truth in a post-death world?

3:    How can there be truth after After?

2:    How can there be truth after the plane went down?

3:    Planes

2:    How can there be truth after all those deaths?

3:    death

2:    How can there be anything at all left that can still, after all this, be considered sacrosanct when we know that planes and death can rain down

3:    reign over

2:    all of us at any moment?

1:    How can there be anything left in a post-world world?

3:    How can't there?

1:    I was doing my washing when I found out

3:    I was walking the dog

2:    I was staring out the window thinking about sex and dinner
      and clean clothes and the kind of noises you make when I give
      you back-rubs and the way you hate flying but you have to do
      it for work and you've managed to work out with terrifying
      accuracy that if you take your drugs right, you could sleep
      through an entire cross-Atlantic flight and I was thinking

3:    The way I always think

1:    About how good or bad it would be to go down in an accident
      while knocked out, about all available evidence and knowledge,
      about whether you would just go from peace to pieces and I
      wonder about how good that could feel and I wonder if you'd
      woken up, if your brain had heard enough to know what was
      happening to send the right chemicals to wake you up or
      something to keep you asleep, keep you calm and out for the
      inevitable, but I guess I'll never be able to ask now because you
      will not be returning home and you don't answer the phone
      anymore

2:    At the time I was just thinking about you.

SCENE: SEDITION

3:    sedition refers to conduct or speech which incites people to
      rebel against the authority of the state

1:    sedition refers to elected state officials conducting themselves
      in a manner which incites people to rebel against the state

2:    sedition is speaking the unspeakable with great accuracy

1:    sedition refers to any peaceful undertakings of any people that
      could lead to any kind of change on any kind of scale that
      could inflict any degree of violence on those who use their
      degrees to sow distrust and hatred between people of a nation

2:    sedition refers to talking shit about your birthplace, the place
      that raised you, the place that made you who you are, caressed
      you and fed you even when you hit back at it

1:    sedition refers to wanting to save your country

2:    sedition refers to wanting to blow up the houses of parliament and everyone in it so you can try to rebuild civil society from any fragile bones of decency that remain

1:    sedition refers to 'rebuilding' and 'burning it down' being the same things

2:    sedition refers to how you feel for your country

3:    *Negaraku, tanah tumpahnya darahku*

       Rakyat hidup bersatu dan maju

       Rahmat bahagia Tuhan kurniakan

       Raja kita selamat bertakhta

       Rahmat bahagia Tuhan kurniakan

       Raja kita selamat bertakhta

2:    My country, my blood spilled on this ground

       1: your country

       2: my wealth

       1: your wealth

       2: my country

       1: your hopes

       2: dreams

       1: Yours

       2: mine

       1: Yours

       2: mine

       1: Yours

       2: Mine

       1: Your words

       2: My downfall

       1: Your words

       2: This country

       1: Your power

       2: This country

1: This fury

3: This furious country

2: I want to love this fury

3: this country

1: this wealth

3: this birth

1: this language

2: this field of blood soaked roses, rosebuds, rose petals covered in the blood of a history that's left us crippled by our own inadequacy to adequately respond to this absolute shambles of democracy

1: and anyway what is democracy if a legal democratic process elects a despot legally anyway

3: if a legal entity allows an illegal action to be legally constituted within a court illegally established and legally continued, has the legal entity fundamentally altered the course of the country to lead down a path of absolute legal collapse?

1: sedition.

3: *Negaraku, tanah tumpahnya darahku*

1: If you spill the blood of a country's people to feed the country, who are you feeding?

2: If you spill your blood to feed a country

3: Blood under sheets

1: Blood under carpets

3: Carpets of leaves and branches rotted by bits of flesh from a woman who could speak in multiple tongues and now speaks in none at all, whose brains now carpet that jungle floor, whose languages now whisper sweet nothings to tiny scuttling critters that understand every single word

1: Shaariibuugiin Altantuuyaa

3: My blood

1: sedition should not in any event be construed as an act of corruption

2:    If you slit open a country and rip out all its secrets and bloodlines

1:    Blood lies

2:    The lies written in blood about the blood that has been spilled

1:    Her blood

2:    If you spill blood to free a country

1:    Her blood

2:    If a country is freed but blood has been spilled

1:    Her blood

2:    /Yours

3:    Should not in any event be construed as an act of corruption

2:    Mine

1:    If this blood you spill of my country

3:    Should not in any event be construed as an act of corruption

1:    Her blood

2:    If I write my name in blood on my country

1:    Her blood

3:    Should not in any event be construed as an act of corruption

1:    If my freedom is spilled in a jungle of silence for a country
      that doesn't remember how to treat blood

2:    Whose freedom has been spilled?

SCENE: WOLF OF PETALING STREET

> *'You know what a "Fugayzi" is?'*
> *'"Fugazi".'*
> *'It's a fake.'*
> *'Fairy dust.'*
> *'It doesn't exist.'*

1:    Let me tell you about power. Real success, real power. It's
      not money or fame or authority. It's the breathlessness of
      knowing that you're doing something something better than
      everyone else around you. It's the weightlessness at the ends of

your fingertips brimming with know-how, with can-do's, with I'm-better-than-all-of-you's. It's the short, bullied kid standing up, pulling out his video camera in one hand, and criminal legislation on assault in the other hand. It's that kid getting the bully arrested and jailed, and then hiring him back as a bodyguard later on minimum wage.

Real power is knowing how to make the system bend around you.

3: It's not malicious or anything.

2: It's just—good. It's just being good at what you do.

3: The inability to *stop* being so

2: Fucking

3: Good

1: Wanting more isn't a sin, it's an expectation

3: How do you turn your life around unless you want to turn your life around?

2: Desperately, absolutely

3: What if you managed to get even the rich to let go of their money?

2: What if you manage to sell to people with money

1: Power is telling someone, a woman, to shave their head for 10,000 dollars in front of an office full of men with their hands down their pants because you know that's not a real choice.

> 'The real question is this—was all this legal?'
> 'Absolutely fucking not.'

2: Bacchanalian plane flights on the way to getting married

3: Training others to have ambition, to do what it takes, to take what they want

1: What's so wrong with making your own way

3: Make your brothers

2: Your sisters

3:    Do what you need them to do?

  'If I took my drugs right, I could sleep through the entire flight.'

2:    It's good for you

3:    Which is good for them

2:    You scratch my back, I scratch yours.

1:    Money talks and power plays and you can hate me but you
  hate me because I'm good, I knew exactly what I was doing.
  My smile, my handshake. Nothing is ever an accident when
  eight zeroes are attached to the end of a number and this was
  no accident, do you think I'm an idiot?

  'You know know what a "Fugayzi" is?'
  'It doesn't exist.'

How do you lose something that big?

Footage from The Wolf of Wall Street *of the yacht capsising intercut with
abstract imagery of people/planes falling through the air.*

1:    Losing power is like this:

VOICEOVER: *Tuan-tuan dan puan-puan, kita telah mendarat di laparan terbang
  antarabangsa KL.*

1:    When it happened, I was thinking about nothing

2:    That peace

3:    That quiet, that absolute bubble, the silence of a million waves,
  billions of networks of oceanic activity

VOICEOVER: *Bagi tujuan keselamatan, anda dikehendaki berada di tempat
  duduk sehingga isyarat 'pasangkan tali keledar' dipadamkan dan pesawat
  berhenti di sepenuhnya.*

3:    Power is forgetting that the higher you go

2:    the more you have to fall when—

3:    and it's always a question of *when*—

2:    the engine cuts out

1:    Everything comes with a price

VOICEOVER: To Malaysians, welcome home.

SCENE: SEARCH / PARTY

Lines in this scene should be delivered in a mix of two languages, possibly Cantonese/English.

1: There, got or not? Anything?

A: *All clear, Captain*

3: Be a bit patient can or not

1: Hungry, lo

3: Want water or not

A: *Guess that's my last piece of fruit for the rest of the year.*

B: *We'll be done and docked all too soon, don't you worry.*

1: Oh my God, why isn't she out yet?

3: Chill, it's just delay la. It *is* Air Asia, you know.

1: True.

   I'm so hungry.

3: There's a banana in the car, if you wait we can 打包 on the way back.

B: *Can you see anything?*

A: *All clear, Captain*

3: Is that her?

   Did she text you?

1: She might not have phone service.

3: There's free Wifi, she's not stupid.

1: Well . . .

3: Don't be mean to your sister.

A: *Captain, I have a ping.*

B: *Do you think maybe—*

A: *It's too soon to tell.*

   It's unlikely but not impossible.

Don't want to get your hopes up.

Changing course now.

3:     Is that her?

1:     Nope, too tall, la

3:     That one?

1:     Not unless she's gotten fugly in the last twelve months.

3:     I don't know how crazy the sun in Australia is

1:     Now who's being mean?

3:     Just in case, prepare first

B: *What do you see?*

A: *Sonar's going fucking crazy, Captain, but it'll take a few minutes for this to settle*

B: *Cut the starboard fans, otherwise we'll spend the rest of the month trying to look through this damn sand.*

A: *Yes, Captain.*

1:     Still not here, ah?

3:     Don't be so annoying, told you to eat dinner first.

1:     Wasn't hungry earlier.

3:     Want McDonald's?

1:     Nah, we can get supper later.

3:     Sit down then, I'm getting a headache from you running around

A: *Captain.*

B: *I see it.*

A: *I'm sorry.*

B: *So am I. Drop the target.*

A: *Should I log it?*

B: *May as well, the scientists'll appreciate it at the very least.*

A: *At least something's thriving down here.*

B: *I'll be in the break room, Ange will be up at 1400.*

A: *Yes, Captain.*

3:   That's her

1:   About time.

     3: Hi, oh my God, baby, how was the flight?

     1: You smell terrible

     2: Sorry, sorry, I started sweating as soon as we landed

     3: Ya, it's crazy today, the haze so bad outside

     2: I just read about it

     3: Did you have to wait for your luggage for a long time

     2: Actually the pilot just couldn't get the plane to line up with the, you know, the exit hallway bit that—

     1: Yeah yeah yeah, okay, let's go, I'm about to starve to death.

     2: Mmm, I kinda need to shit actually.

     1: Oh my God, why didn't you do that on the plane?

     2: Uh, privacy? I didn't feel like it?

     1: Okay, can we grab food on the way back though?

     2: Not unless you want me to shit in the car.

     1: Okay, gross.

     2: Sorry, thought if I actually did that it'd be worse, so.

     1: Ew.

     3: I'm glad you're back.

     1: I'm not.

     2: Ha. ha.

B: *Stay sharp and get back on course.*
     We might still find it.

A: *Captain?*
     Do you really believe that?
     Captain?

SCENE: SHAME

2:    take the call

take off the bells and whistles

see the body beneath

see the flesh and bone

the wrinkles and the blemishes

the creases, joyful and not

place fingertips gently on eyelids, soft and not-fluttering

slowly, slowly

cover the eyes

cover the truths they will never recount again from their hollow cheeks

cover the hands under a sheet

the smell of clean, fresh, detergent

the smell of

jet fuel

a non-smell full of possibilities of the could've beens

3: Doctor

1: Accountant

3: Teacher

1: Politician

3: Thief

1: Happy family, three kids

3: Happy family, one son, one wife, domineering, public, powerful

1: Happy family, no kids, two dogs, judgmental clucking aunties

2:    The wake:

1: I remember when your hair was longer

3: I remember when your skirt was longer

1: I remember when your responses to your grandma were longer

3: When you spoke more Hokkien

1: When you spoke more Malay

3: When you spoke more

1: You used to be so polite, now you just say everything you're thinking

3: A bit of respect would go a long way

2: If you like it so much there then why don't you stay there?

3: Watch the flames rise

1: Wash your hands in 982°C heat

3: Temperatures so high the body is vaporised

2: Cremation

3: Flesh melts off bone, hair chars, skin burns

1: Throw in your resentment for luck

2: Fire crackles, hot and clean

1: Toss in the shame you feel about where you came from and where you want to go

2: Haha, yeah, no, my parents don't really like gay people

3: Brown people

1: Black people

3: Chinese people

1: Poor people

3: Fat people

1: Ugly people

3: People coming over

1: People who spit

3: People who have tattoos

1: People who don't spend a lot of money

3: People who spend too much money

1: People who don't like travelling

3: People who travel too much

1: People who drink

3: People who don't drink

1/2/3: It's just how they were raised

1: Haha, yeah, no, she moved here just before I was born and didn't have any friends so she kind of just stayed home. Yeah, some of her friends come over and she hangs out with them, I don't really know what they talk about, they usually speak in Hakka.

3: Haha, yeah, no, they think the Greens are hippies who live in tents.

1: Haha, yeah, no, he takes photos of every single dish of food when we go on tour, they spend more time getting people to take photos of them with the view than they spend actually looking at the view

3: Haha, yeah, no, they don't like using the self-checkout because it's a bit stressful, they might press the wrong button

1: Haha, yeah, no, they just don't like being in the sun

3: Haha, yeah, no, of course, yeah

3: Let your shame burn

1: Let your name burn

3: Let your family burn

2: rest in peace.

SCENE: BECAUSE

2: songs about leaving

1: poems about leaving

3: TV shows about leaving

2: people who leave because they can't stay anymore

1: people who can't stay anymore can't stay anymore because they're sick

2: sick at heart

3: sick in the head

2: sick of being

1: sick of being gay

3: sick of being smart

2: sick of being

3: feared

1: political footballs

2: sick of making excuses for other people

3: when I was five I—

1: when I was eight I saw—

2: when I was twenty-one I tried to—

1/2/3: /I

2: and then you realise it really doesn't matter what happened because you can't change it and every time you bring it up you fight so you've stopped bringing it up but you know it lingers and he knows it's lingering and they linger

but anyway it doesn't matter because at the end of the day you've just got what you have left

anyway

2: I didn't leave because I was—

3: Different

1: Bored

3: Rich

1: Poor

3: Angry

1: Lost

2:   I left because I could

3:   because I want you to deal with your problems by becoming
     rich

1:   I left because I knew it was easier to leave and live

2:   And I wanted to live so badly but I'd run out of reasons

3:   I couldn't let myself go on dying

1:   Dying in conversations I found inane and pointless

3:   Dying from shots fired by people too stupid to realise that they
     were shooting themselves in the foot the entire time

1:   Too bribed-up to realise

3:   Too—

1:   to not be construed as an act of corruption

2:   To care

3:   I wanted to be able to leave the house without feeling like I
     might get murdered walking out the door

1:   I wanted to be able to wear whatever I wanted to wear and not
     get called 'sir'

3:   To not get catcalled

1:   To not get called

3:   To not get

2:   To forget

3:   I wanted to bury myself under new layers and call it change

1:   I left because it was exhausting

2:   I left because I was exhausted

1:   I left because I couldn't stay anymore

3:   I left because some planes just weren't made to land

2:   Leaving is such sweet sorrow

1:   A deficiency in the amount of oxygen reaching the heart

2:   I left because I could so I did and I regret it but I'd do it
     again and again and again anyway given the chance because

whatever happened after that all I got from leaving and all I lost from staying here could never compare to what I knew I wasn't feeling when I was staying so anyway I'm still not quite right here but if I hadn't left I don't know what I would've done so I just

3:    Left.

2:    I'm sorry.

SCENE: TELL-ALL 2

3:    can you hear me?

hello, can you hear me?

it's just about the

sorry

so

1:    yes

3:    you're saying that

1:    yes

3:    based on all available evidence and knowledge

1:    all the available evidence yes

3:    based on your years of experience and knowledge and evidence and know-how and expertise

1:    yes

3:    based on all of that, what you are saying to me now is that

1:    yes

3:    that my

1:    yes

3:    that my daughter is not, she will not be

1:    yes

3:    she will not be returning home

1:    yes

3:     to me

1:     yes

3:     I see

1:     I'm sorry for your

2:     your loss.

3:     thank you.

SCENE: SURRENDER

1:     So we end up back at

3:     pistol shrimp

1:     blood

3:     cavitation bubbles

1:     military sonar picking up all the wrong signals

3:     sending home all the wrong signals

1:     benevolent gods and unintelligent machines

3:     lost money

1:     lost plane

3:     the smell of jet fuel

1:     the smell of *nasi lemak*

3:     falling

1:     flying

A scream with no sound in it. Mournful.

2:     when you wake up to the taste of a scream on the edge of your
       teeth when you wake up in a country full of people feeling
       like no-one else exists or maybe you've stopped existing for
       anyone else when you reach inside your guts and all that's
       there is the smell of jet fuel when your heart pounds in your
       ears like flight and you know it's too late to run you're in too
       deep you put yourself too deep you got too involved when you
       wake and you're drenched in sweat-fear-tears someone else's

hot corpse breath on your ear try to piece the nightmare back together because if you can make sense of it then it will stop scaring you and next time next time next time you can pull at the strands and the entire thing will unravel so easily unravel like it doesn't matter and then maybe you can stop fighting because you'll forget what you were running from in the first place so you won't be scared anymore and you could be anyone, do anything

SCENE: FAMILY DINNER 3

Silence. Silence then noise—the clink of utensils, distant. A revolving wooden tabletop, a quiet hum.

SOUND: SOS being tapped out in Morse code, or with the clicking of pistol shrimp. It slows to the rhythm of a heartbeat.

Silence.

1: If a plane falls into the middle of the ocean and kills 8,000 pistol shrimp and no-one is there to see it.

3: If 680 million ringgit is deposited into a hidden bank account and no-one finds it.

2: If a girl leaves a country and no-one notices it happening.

3: If no-one tries to stop it.

1: If no-one heard about it.

2: Did it happen?

THE END